Poetic
for the sake of feeling

poetry written by
Rachel White • Chelsea Todd • Aishvarya T

Copyright © 2024 Rachel White, Chelsea Todd and Aishvarya T

Mildura, Australia

All rights reserved.

ISBN: **978-0-6456064-4-7**
Imprint: Independently Published

Poetic
for the sake of feeling

poetry written by
Rachel White + Chelsea Todd + Aishvarya T

In sorrow and solace, I look to the sky wondering how much more I can take, that is when I realised, it was all for feelings sake.

for the sake of feeling anger	11
for the sake of feeling joy	19
for the sake of feeling disgust	27
for the sake of feeling love	35
for the sake of feeling sadness	43
for the sake of feeling peace	51
for the sake of feeling envy	59
for the sake of feeling surprise	67
for the sake of feeling fear	75
for the sake of feeling the sunshine and the storm	83

Preface

Three poets gathered each week, for the sake of writing, for the sake of expression, for the sake of feeling. Connecting inwards and proceeding to allow the oceanic depths within them to pour out onto these pages. Reciting, refining the edges, and most importantly preparing to share with you.

Poetry has the power to express what often goes unsaid in our daily world, and in a way that cuts directly to the emotional core. In our poetic expression we can bypass the mind's sneaky tendency to rationalise our feelings. We can be as dramatic, delusional, or ridiculous as we feel the need to be in that moment. We can create a safe space for our sorrow and find solace in the art we create because of our pain. We can also immortalise our joy so that the afterglow remains for others to feel.

All three of us are poets because we chose to sit down and write. You have a poet within you too. We hope that these words resonate with different parts of you and inspire a deeper connection with your feelings, or the outpouring of your own poetic musings.

Read slowly.

Pause between the pieces.

All for the sake of feeling.

for the sake of feeling anger

She was the flames of the fire, from the ashes she arose
She arrived in this moment to dissolve, destroy or explode
Doing all the things that you don't have the heart to do
She clears the way for all of your breakthroughs
Her love, in actuality, is so wildly immense
So she bears the burden of all your judgements
And loves you through your harsh defence

Feel her warmth before she burns you down
Reject her and you will bear witness to ashes all around
You cannot destroy her, for from those ashes she will always rise
She lives in your forever flame burning from inside.

By Rachel White

'Sugar and spice and all things nice,
That's what little girls are made of…'
The rhyme sung from her Mother's sweet lips
As she cradled into her lap
'You were such a good girl'
Sweet, quiet and kind
{taming the wild song in her mind}

And this sweet good girl
Grew into her long gangly legs
Her hips became fuller
Her load even fuller
Perfection overtook her
Striving shook her
Guilt pushed her
Until cracks appeared

Beneath the sweet icing
And strawberry kissed lips
Sacred rage grew like
A foam rapid of beaten egg whites
Roaring to the shore of her existence
Unstoppable fury
Crashing
With force imprinted on the gentle sands of childhood
Where she searched for shells at sunset

Waves she was too afraid to ride
Without her Mother by her side
As she stepped into the ocean alone
What was unseen became known
The facade of the perfect mother
Dissolved by the crashing water
She realised she had become her

By Chelsea Todd

Anger for the little girls,
who're told to be good to be liked.

Anger for the women,
whose bodies are constantly objectified.

Anger for the mother,
who constantly feels she is behind.

Anger for the corporate girlie,
who feels she's gotta hustle all the time.

Anger for the social media,
where people feel compelled to pretend life's great.

Anger for the world,
where women don't feel beautiful or safe.

Anger, or should I say, sorrow
for the society we live in.

Do I even dare to hope,
that things can one day change from being so grim?

By Aishvarya T

for the sake of feeling joy

Sunshine, oh sunshine
Come with me to play
Dancing in your light
Keeps my dreams awake

Your warmth, it envelops me
Makes me feel that I could fly
Like just my peaceful breath
Could lift me into the sky

Joy, oh joy
I'll call you by your name
You tickle me with happiness
And your afterglow remains

By Rachel White

Sunshine soothing down to the bone
Cherished souls who feel like home

Lemonade, lemonade
Fizz and pop

Springy sponge cake
With a cherry on top

Peaches, peaches
Juice down your cheek

Storytelling by the campfire
And the sweet nothings we speak.

By Chelsea Todd

To the little girl, who believed
her dad was a superhero.

The little girl, who believed
that christmases were real

The girl who believed her first love,
was her happily ever after.

The girl who believed in true love,
in spite of heartbreaks.

The girl who fought to see,
the rainbow in every storm.

The girl who chose,
to pick herself up after every fall.

The girl who became,
her own superhero woman.

The kind of superhero,
who'd have made the little girl proud.

May your kind grow and shine
May your delusion truly become the solution
As you are creating a life worthy of celebration.

By Aishvarya T

for the sake of feeling disgust

I dropped my pen just before writing this
Like my body couldn't help but to resist
It didn't want to un-bury this truth
But I picked up my pen and let my hand move
So if writing this I must
Let's explore my feelings of disgust
The recoiling of my skin
The repulsion of my being
The vile thoughts I hide
Just so I can get by
It takes a lot not to show you
So pretend is all that I can do
For it's all that I can see
When I see you look at me
And it isn't supposed to be this way
The boat has sailed on things to say
You should have built a better image
But I'm afraid you can't repair this damage
I feel disgusted when I look at you
Because that's how you made me feel about my mirror's view

By Rachel White

They say we reap what we sow
For a time I believed that
But now…
I don't know

As a Maiden I gave everything my all
Dawn til dusk and beyond I'd toil
Giving and achieving until my cup was empty
Delusions that my energy was plenty

Amongst all the hustle and go-go-go
I lost my divine feminine flow
Climbed the ladder oh so high
While my womb was empty and vessel dry

Beyond the veil shame would hide
Invisible pain and longing buried inside
Believing birthing a child is a womanly must
To be 'barren' felt like a cloak of disgust

At last my soul baby heard me calling
My belly grew rounder and my masks started falling
I share my story to give shame a home
In the hope other women don't feel so alone.

By Chelsea Todd

The boys on the streets,
making lewd comments on the girls.
The heartless non humans,
raping and murdering women.

People who lie and betray,
the ones going back on their word,
the ones with ill intentions
taking joy from the pain they've stirred.

The faceless humans,
who stoop to despicable lows,
when they know their face,
isn't going to be shown.

My stomach twists in disgust,
a sour, bitter taste
Your presence reeks of distrust,
a waste of space.

Revulsion fills the room,
heavy and thick.
The mirror wishes to cease to exist,
the moment you see it.

By Aishvarya T

for the sake of feeling love

The slow beats within my chest
The peaceful embrace where I can rest
The encompassing light of the unknown
This is the love that I call home
With threads tied across time and space
Interwoven beautifully to the human race
Love is gentle, love is loud
Love is the answer, just look around
Love is our salvation, our home
It's how we know we aren't ever alone
This love, this life, a gift from above
That's how we can be sure that we are always enough

By Rachel White

Wishing on stars
And singing my longing
Waves of my heart
Seeking belonging

Conceived as the sweetest, smallest seed
Nurturing dearly your every need

Hearts in harmony
Your resonance imprints on my womb
Even when it seems there's no more room
My heart expands and more love blooms

From ocean deep and skies above
We'll meet under the tree entwined in love.

By Chelsea Todd

Sun on my skin,
sand beneath my feet,
wind in my hair,
waves twirling to a beat.

Ice lolly in my hands,
rose petals strewn all around,
carried away by the gentle tide,
going along for the ride.

Wedding altar behind my back,
the groom who chose another track,
the guests taken aback,
but, I don't give a crack.

Because it doesn't matter,
because I finally get it.
Love is what I already have,
love is what I already am.

By Aishvarya T

for the sake of feeling sadness

Sometimes it creeps up on me
Caressing across my heart like a wave
Washing over all the sore points
The parts of me still waiting to be saved
When it catches me off guard, the waves take me away
Pulling me out into the deep
Floating so far adrift
That now it's only sadness that I see.

But there's nothing to attach it to
This sorrow that I feel
So I float and I wonder
How much of it is real.

And then the revelation dawns
That this ocean is full with my own tears
It was my heart that caught them
To keep the sadness near

This ocean holds depth
In the way that it flows
Waiting for me to see the beauty in it
Nowhere else for my sadness to go

By Rachel White

Paintings and drawings frame the walls
I can almost imagine hearing your calls... "Mummmm..."

Silence dances on clean floorboards
And knocks quietly at your closed bedroom door

Stuffed toys sleep soundly in your blanket box
Among your treasures and mislaid socks

The sometimes longed for silence in the Motherhood haze
Is now cradled and rocked as I count the days

I trust you are nurtured with your Dad
When you're back in my arms I'll say I love you, not that I'm sad.

By Chelsea Todd

Raindrops falling, mild breeze blowing,
as I sit watching the crashing waves on the sea.
Not a soul in sight, just the endless tide,
much like the storm I hold inside.

Ears start ringing, throat almost choking,
chest clenching, floor seems to be spinning,
my silent cries turn to screams,
my tears competing with the torrential rain,
as the floodgates of my heart bleed open,
letting out all the pain.

No words, no thoughts, no one to explain,
just my bleeding heart, crying out in vain.
Wind muffling my screams,
rain washing my tears,
the moon my only witness
of this sadness I can hardly bear.

By Aishvarya T

for the sake of feeling peace

Oh, what would I give?
What would I be willing to be,
To be the light of the peace
In this chaotic journey?

What would it take, for peace, for me to be
How could it take anything, except for being me?

The chaotic will be coherent
The storm will turn to still
The tormented will be torn down
The emptiness will be refilled

The cycle will continue
Peace amongst it all
At the centre emanating outward
For me to sit here and recall

By Rachel White

Deep inhale, slow release
Arriving in a place of peace

Golden sand and turquoise sea
A home that grounds and centres me

Each squeaky grain holds life's noise
Anchors angst and turns chaos to poise

Rollings waves rise and subside
Like life's challenges and shifting tide

Sometimes turbulent, sometimes calm
By the sea my worries disarm.

By Chelsea Todd

As i walk out of the room,
holding my own

No anger or resentment,
over the pain I was shown.

Choosing my peace over,
what people would say,

Choosing to let go over,
the desire to make him pay.

Smiling at the joke of it all,
as all along the key was just me.

My decision to choose peace,
and the decision to choose me.

By Aishvarya T

for the sake of feeling envy

Colour me green and what do I see?
The kids having fun who don't want to play with me
The ones who it comes easy to, to believe,
That they were worthy of the magic that life could be.

If I have to be jealous
For a moment I'll admit
I'm envious of the people who can just up and quit
Those who don't think things through or have a care
Those who have outrageous thoughts that they share

It may be in our nature to compare.

Gazing over the fence illuminates everything that I am not
It becomes obvious in that moment what I have forgot
So thank you envy for this reminder
For being the portal back to my own garden to tender

By Rachel White

Green, green
Lingering
Tinged with blue, achy longing

Sparkling on the surface, grounded on the beach
Swim deeper, smiles hide what's beyond reach

Green, green
Simmering
Dreams not realised, sights unseen

Bubbling, brewing in the pot
Desire grows, blessings are forgot

Green, green
Forrest deep
Lost in thoughts of seeds you never got to reap

Envy in all shades of green
Coloured tales unwritten in the space in between.

By Chelsea Todd

I look around and see,
a world as unfair as could be.
Dad's little princesses,
their every whim catered to.
People who have it easy,
luck always favours their side.
People who've hit the jackpot,
loving family along for the ride.

Why can't that be me?
The girl who can ask for what she wants,
because there are people to give it to her.
The girl who can finally take a break,
because there are people who have her back.
Why do I have to always be the one holding my life upright?
Why can't I be her?
At least for a day...
Why can't I be her?
Don't I deserve a break?

By Aishvarya T

for the sake of feeling surprise

That glance, you caught my eye
I was transported to the depths of the universe inside
Oh, it was a wild ride
To see the stars so alight
To feel the milky way move so bright
To taste Venus in delight
To gaze at Saturn and admire its size
Oh, that moment when you caught my eye
It sure did take me by surprise
I could have never imagined how alive I would feel in your mind
I wouldn't have guessed our souls had met before and travelled through time

Yes indeed, it was a surprise
When I blinked and you were gone and I realised
We haven't met yet in this life

Don't worry my darling I remember your eyes
No matter your face those I'lll recognise
I look forward to this expected surprise.

By Rachel White

Dazzling sea and shining sun
A little girl has just turned one
Splashing and digging by the tide
Cool water licks and tickles, eyes delight open wide

Balmy nights and sunsets from heaven
A little girl of magic seven
Collecting shells, treasures and strewn things
An empty bottle - cave for an octopus with aztec rings!

Summer days stretch beyond the sea
Wise and innocent at thirteen
Clasped hands, sweet kiss
Sundrenched unexpected bliss

Lingering by the sea
Lovers, best friends, both twenty
Deep blue eyes, sweet romance
Glassy water breaks as dolphins dance

Wintery beach stroll, nowhere to be
Holding her hands he drops to one knee
Salty tears and sparkling eyes
Harmony of delighted love and surprise

Dazzling sea and shining sun
Two little boys, three and one
Splashing and digging as the day rises
Blessed with life's divine plans and surprises

By Chelsea Todd

Moved into my new home, all alone.
How's it gonna be? I don't know.

New country, new people, everything's unknown.
Why do I have to do this all alone?

Wandering the empty rooms, dead inside.
The hollow hallways echo the emptiness I hide.

Surprised by the bell who could it be?
OMG, my bestie from a different country!

Is this for real, I couldn't believe,
mouth wide open, eyes locked in their sleeve

Walking around, not leaving her side,
staring at her, with a grin so wide.

Still can't believe my own eyes,
she had brought me back to life..

By Aishvarya T

for the sake of feeling fear

I heard him, I swear
The monster over there
Hiding in the dark corner
Creeping closer and closer
His warm and eerie breath on my neck
Too afraid to open my eyes and check
But I know the monster is near
He's picking up my pillow to smother me with fear
I'm hiding under the blanket holding on for life's dear
My eyes stay closed so I can't see him clear

Whole body flushed with scarlet red
Who will find me in the morning dead?
All alone, nowhere else to hide or go
Monster get it over with, stop going slow

A single thought drops in so bright
What if I were to turn on the light?

Paralysed... I can't seem to move.
What else to fear will I let myself lose?

By Rachel White

Freeze
Snake
Silently slithering across the stony path
Stalling several seconds
Sliding under the white weatherboard house
Disappearing into darkness
Destined to surface sometime mysteriously

Freeze
Speak
Words swirling in her head
Stuck in her throat
Suspended in sticky classroom air
Disassociated, silence except for a slow clock strum
Snickering lips framed by thirty-six scrutinising eyes

Year by year
Brick by brick
She built an imagined wall of safety
Hiding from the fear of being seen
Fear of persecution
Fear of embracing the power of her fullest expression
Waiting for the snake to stir from slumber

Words unspoken wove like red threads into her hips
Silent stories simmered amber spells in her cauldron
The fire in her belly bubbled up glowing golden
Heart song swelled like a wave's green room
Bountiful blue words spilled out, serenading souls who could see
Inner knowing crystallised into indigo dreams
Rising to conquer fear and greet the violet sky

By Chelsea Todd

He sneaks up on me,
when I least expect.
My old dreaded friend,
I thought i'd forget

Cold clammy fingers,
slowly creeping over my skin.
Like fast growing shadows,
by the sun setting in

Heart rate rises,
breath coming up short,
dry throat closes,
I feel my stomach drop.

So familiar, but i'm frozen in shock,
paralysed in place, by my own thoughts,
cold fist of fear, holding me in its familiar clasp,
I stand stuck, a prisoner in the pause.

By Aishvarya T

for the sake of feeling the sunshine and the storm

I long to dance in the storm
To cry under the glow of the sun
To be present with the world
With nature to be one.

I flow like the river
I am strong like the stone
I bloom in cycles like the flower
Like the wind I sense where I am to go

I'll cry an ocean and have my tears wiped by the sun
I'll play in the rain, even enjoy pain
For I know it be to sacred every single day

Just as I am one with the earth
The oceans, the people, the entire universe
So too are the rays of sunshine and all the storms
Part of the same story - I'll embrace it all.

By Rachel White

Silver lined clouds
Rainbows after rain
Calm before storms
Splashed with pleasure and pain

She's only happy in the sun
Dancing with diamonds on her shoes
Worthy when she's winning
A game of life we'll one day lose

Eating juicy peaches
From the lushest trees
Discarding spotty apples
Only perfect please

Here comes the rain again
Lightning crashes, purple rain pours down
Riders on the storm
The Queen adjusts her crown

I see you, darling
Taking shelter from the storm
But here comes the sun
No need to stay forlorn

Have you ever seen the rain?
Life's not an endless Summer of sunshine and butterflies
Stormy seasons, endings and cocooning
Clear the path to explore blue skies.

By Chelsea Todd

I stand helpless watching,
as she razes everything to the ground.
Her fury unmatching,
all the foundations,I thought will stay around.

I stand too shocked,
watching my life fall apart.
Oddly still feeling calm,
at least, I can see who won't last.

But, from the rubble of my destroyed dreams
emerged a future I couldn't have seen.
I discovered a whole new me,
Filled with courage, no matter what may seem.

For every night leads to dawn,
every storm tends to calm,
and life always goes on,
for those who face it head on.

By Aishvarya T

Now it is your turn to write. Open the page, pick up your pen, take a breath, soften your body, and allow what is on your heart to pour out with your ink. There is no pressure to write anything profound, write only for feeling sake.

When we wrote we would set a ten-minute timer to allow our initial channelled draft to pour out. Simply let yourself write and know you can refine and flesh out further later.

The first step in becoming a poet is by allowing yourself to write. The more you write, the more at ease you will feel expressing your poetic musings in writing. There is so much depth within you. We would love for you to share it with us and the world.

for the sake of feeling anger

for the sake of feeling joy

for the sake of feeling disgust

for the sake of feeling love

for the sake of feeling sadness

for the sake of feeling peace

for the sake of feeling envy

for the sake of feeling surprise

for the sake of feeling fear

for the sake of feeling the sunshine and the storm

About the writers

Rachel White is an author, poet and artist of life. Her art and services aim to connect women with their own true essence, depth, and full expression. Rachel draws on a depth of embodied study and experiences to create in the realms of creativity, poetry, spirituality, feminine energy, and making life a true work of art.

IG - @byrachelwhite

Chelsea Todd is a healer, intuitive, yoga practitioner, writer and Mother. Her dharma (life's work) is to share the medicine of words, psychology, and yoga to guide others to a deeper connection with themselves, those they love and the world. Her nurturing energy holds space for others in an empowering way.

IG - @ drchelseatodd

Aishvarya T started her poetic journey with her debut collection, drawing readers into the emotional landscapes of love and connection. Her latest collection continues the exploration of emotions. Beyond the page, she connects with audiences through her podcast on mindset and spirituality, empowering others to live with intention.

IG - @inksensebyaishu

www.ingramcontent.com/pod-product-compliance
Lightning Source LLC
Chambersburg PA
CBHW022019290426
44109CB00015B/1229